Five Steps to Unmask the Real You... Before Relationships Damage You!

Five Steps to Unmask the Real You Copyright © 2020 by Author Tamera Kelly. All Rights Reserved.

All rights reserved. No part of this book may be reproduced in any form or by any electronic or mechanical means including information storage and retrieval systems, without permission in writing from the author. The only exception is by a reviewer, who may quote short excerpts in a review.

Cover designed by Cover Designer

Author Tamera Kelly
Visit my website at www.atkelly.com

Printed in the United States of America

First Printing: July 2020
Amazon/KDP

ISBN-13 : 978-1-7354394-2-6

"One life is enough to question all truths, yet the only lie that remains profound is the lie that you tell yourself about you."

Step 1:

Representative

Step 1: Representative

It doesn't matter where you go in life, you will always meet an individual's representative first. Be mindful of the image that you portray due to there is always an opportunist waiting and willing to take you up
on your offer.

Using your wealth and body to obtain attention always attract the wrong attention. Sex and money will always go hand into hand. However, morals, ethics, and values will never need distinction. You attract what you seek, and an individual should be able to gain the opposite sex attention with their clothes on and financial status undisclosed.

My Representative

What image do you portray to others?

_____
_____
_____
_____
_____

What are your morals, ethics, and values?

_____
_____
_____
_____
_____

Step 2: Can I Trust You?

Step 2: Can I Trust You?

If you can't be honest with yourself, you **will** damage every individual who comes in contact romantically with you. No one asks to be lied to. The truth should always be told regardless of the outcome. Trust is fragile, easily broken, and hard to attain once it is broken. Thus, being the two reasons why we don't trust people: (1) We don't know them and (2) We know them. Therefore, having a good thing is so hard and meeting a strong person IS so rare.

At the end of the day, everyone isn't deserving of the love that you have to offer. People no longer desire something real and complaints are reasons to make excuses avoidable. Be at peace with that and honest with yourself. In life, as an individual, you have to love and value yourself first. You have to analyze your assets (mental, physical, emotional, and spiritual) in your entirety before requesting someone to invest in you. It's imperative to possess the qualities that you seek before seeking investors due to liabilities causing casualties and no one wants to deal with the aftermath of unnecessary damage.

Can I Trust Me?
Are you honest with yourself?

_____

_____

_____

_____

_____

What are your assets?

_____

_____

_____

_____

_____

Step 3: Self-Reflection

Step 3: Self-Reflection

Self-Reflection is the hardest conversation an individual will have in their life. It's hard to remove a mask that you have mastered the design, patented it, and sized perfectly to fit your... Representative.

Stop looking for people to validate you. If what you bring to the table isn't accepted; Excuse yourself from the table and never be afraid to eat alone. You weren't created for everyone which means everyone isn't going to enjoy what you serve. However, serve your menu anyway. The individual that is right for you will meet you halfway and help you prepare a meal fit for the kingdom. Don't start eating lies just because your heart is hungry and never go back for leftovers when you were never invited for dinner. Consuming an unbalanced diet will surely leave you with a ton of shit.

Self-Reflection

Are you still wearing your mask?

_____

_____

_____

_____

_____

What are your eating habits?

_____

_____

_____

_____

_____

Step 4: Unpack Your Bags

Step 4: Unpack Your Bags

Life is entirely too short to make irrelevant situations relevant. Living and coexisting are two separate entities. You have to learn how to live and enjoy your life due to you only receiving one. Everything doesn't deserve your attention nor response. Some situations are visible for you to see for you to know and grow. Never force what doesn't fit due to this: Unhealthy Practices create Unhealthy Perceptions. Sometimes you have to put aside what you feel for them, and pay attention to what their actions are saying they feel for you due to; you can give someone the world and in return not have a place in it. Therefore, single and waiting is better than taken and faking.

Unpack Your Bags
Are you living or coexisting?

_____
_____
_____
_____
_____
_____

What unhealthy practices created unhealthy perceptions for you?

_____
_____
_____
_____
_____

Step 5: Time Out

Step 5: Time Out

Live each day of your life with a purpose while never regretting a decision that you consciously made. For at that moment, that was something you wanted to do. Therefore, love and forgive yourself wholeheartedly and freely while allowing tomorrow to take care of itself. You can't lose what you never had, can't keep what isn't yours, and can't hold on to something that does not want to stay. When dealing with a breakup, it is essential to take the necessary time out for you to heal completely. This process is necessary to go through due to your mental and emotional well-being during that time.

Oftentimes, people jump into one relationship to the next under false pretenses trying to fulfill a void without reading the "Caution" label, which in return ends up creating more resentment and disrespect for the opposite sex. There isn't a manual on how to deal with a breakup due to individuals dealing with situations differently. Therefore, you must take the necessary time to fall back in love with yourself while reevaluating your mental stability. It is extremely easy to lose yourself while appeasing others and, if you don't catch yourself, you will end up mentally relinquishing your rights to be yourself.

Time Out
Have you forgiven yourself?

_____
_____
_____
_____
_____

Are you ignoring the caution label?

_____
_____
_____
_____
_____

Notes

Notes

Notes

Notes

Notes

Notes

www.ingramcontent.com/pod-product-compliance
Lightning Source LLC
Chambersburg PA
CBHW060808090426
42736CB00002B/197